Contents

A self-portrait of Van Gogh, painted in 1889

Vincent van Gogh

Brandon Robshaw
and
Rochelle Scholar

Published in association with The Basic Skills Agency

Hodder & Stoughton

A MEMBER OF THE HODDER HEADLINE GROUP

Acknowledgements

Cover: Fred van Deelen

'Self-portrait', AKG photo/Musée d'Orsay, Paris, p. iv;

'Sunrise over young corn', AKG photo/Staatliche Graphische Sammlung, p. 2;

'The Church at Auvers-sur-Oise', AKG photo/Musée d'Orsay, Paris, p. 9;

'The Potato Eaters', AKG photo/Rijksmuseum Vincent van Gogh, p. 14;

'Terrace of the cafe in the evening', AKG photo/Collection Emery Reves, p. 17;

'Sunflowers', AKG photo/Christie's London, p. 20;

'Self-portrait with ear cut off', AKG photo/Private Collection, p. 23.

Orders: please contact Bookpoint Ltd, 39 Milton Park, Abingdon, Oxon OX14 4TD. Telephone: (44) 01235 400414, Fax: (44) 01235 400454. Lines are open from 9.00–6.00, Monday to Saturday, with a 24 hour message answering service. Email address: orders@bookpoint.co.uk

British Library Cataloguing in Publication Data
A catalogue record for this title is available from The British Library

ISBN 0 340 74266 6

First published 1999
Impression number   10 9 8 7 6 5 4 3 2 1
Year   2004 2003 2002 2001 2000 1999

Copyright © 1999 Brandon Robshaw and Rochelle Scholar

Typeset by Fakenham Photosetting Ltd, Fakenham, Norfolk.
Printed in Great Britain for Hodder & Stoughton Educational, a division of Hodder Headline Plc, 338 Euston Road, London NW1 3BH by Redwood Books, Trowbridge, Wiltshire.

1 Crows Above a Cornfield

The painting was finished.
Vincent looked at his work.
The yellow field of corn.
Black crows rising above it.
The deep blue sky.
The burning yellow sun.

Vincent picked up his brush.
He wrote 'Crows Above a Cornfield'
in the corner of the painting.

The year was 1890.
It was midday. The middle of July.
The middle of a field in France.
There was no sound.
The yellow field of corn
shimmered in the heat haze.
The sun beat down on the back of his neck.

Vincent felt tired and ill.
He could not go on.
He could not stand living any more.
He had suffered enough.

'Sunrise over young corn', painted in 1889

He looked at his painting again.
Would anyone buy it?
He did not know.
He did not care.

He took the gun out of his pocket.
He looked up to the burning yellow sun.
He pressed the gun to his side
and pulled the trigger.
The gunshot rang out.
Black crows rose into the deep blue sky.
Vincent fell to the earth.
Red blood stained the yellow corn.

The sun beat down.
Four hours passed.
Vincent groaned.
Another failure.
He couldn't even kill himself.

He pressed his hand to his side.
He staggered to his feet.
He had to get help.
He had to find his friends.

2 Shadows of the Past

The dark red blood stained his clothes.
With each step
he could feel life ebbing away.
The sun burnt down on his head.

Just a few more steps.
Then he would be back at the cafe.

He felt afraid.
Would he live or die?

He fell through the doors of the cafe.

'Oh, Vincent, Vincent, what have you done?'
said the owner.
He sent for Vincent's friend, a doctor.

'Vincent, why did you do it?' asked the doctor.
'There is so much more for you to do.
Your work is not finished yet.'

Vincent couldn't answer him.
He closed his eyes.

It was dark and cool in his room.
The doctor sat with Vincent until night came.
The candles were lit and
shadows on the wall flickered.

Vincent looked at the shadows.
They looked like faces.
Faces of people he had met in his life.
Maybe they were coming back to say goodbye.

Vincent closed his eyes.
He wanted to remember the past.
He wanted to remember for the last time.

3 The Early Years

The darkness of his room in France faded.
Vincent remembered his life in London.

It was 1874. Vincent was 21.
He worked for an art dealer, selling prints,
and he had fallen in love for the first time.

The woman he loved was called Ursula.
And she was beautiful.

Vincent had red hair and deep set eyes.
He looked strong.
He was not a handsome man.
He always felt so clumsy.

He begged Ursula to marry him.
But she was engaged to marry someone else.
She said she could never love Vincent.
because he was 'a red-headed fool'.

Vincent left his job and went back to Holland
to live with his parents.
But he could not stop thinking about Ursula.
In the end, he went back to England.
He got a job as a teacher in Ramsgate.

Every weekend,
he would walk all the way to London
and stand outside Ursula's house.

Then, one weekend, he saw
a carriage outside the house.
Ursula came out in a wedding dress.
She was holding her father's arm.
She was on her way to get married.

Heartbroken, Vincent left England for
Amsterdam to stay with his uncle.
What was he going to do with his life?

4 Life with the Miners

Vincent decided to work for the Church
and help the poor and sick.
In 1877, he went to a college in Belgium
to learn how to be a preacher.
But he did not get on with the teacher.
He was too shy to read out his work in class.
The words stuck in his throat.

Vincent failed the course.
Another failure.
Was his whole life going to be like this?

But one of the priests took pity on Vincent.
He asked if Vincent would be a preacher
to the coal miners in Belgium.

When Vincent first saw the miners,
he was shocked.
Men, women and children
worked in the mines.
They lived in huts.
They suffered from cold, hunger and fever.
The area was covered in coal smoke.
The trees were dead and black.

'The Church at Auvers-sur-Oise', painted in 1890

Vincent wanted to share
the miners' suffering.
He lived in a hut like them.
He ate the same bad food as they did.
He suffered from the same fevers.
He wore the same shabby clothes.
He even rubbed coal dust on his face
to look like them.

One day, there was a terrible accident
in the mine.
57 miners were buried alive.
As Vincent held a memorial service for them,
some priests from the college arrived
to check on him.
They were shocked by his shabby clothes
and dirty face.
They said he was a disgrace to the church
and sacked him on the spot.

Vincent was 26 years old
and had failed at everything he had tried.
He was poor. The bad food
and unhealthy conditions had made him ill.
He lived alone in his dirty little shack.
He became very depressed.

5 'You are an artist, Vincent.'

Vincent would go out walking
for hours and hours.
He would look at the fields,
the peasants, the woods.
Everything was covered in coal dust.
Something inside Vincent
made him want to draw what he saw.

He had never had lessons in drawing.
He thought his drawings were terrible.
But they had something.
A sense of life.
A sense of energy.

Drawing helped Vincent
to come out of his depression.
His brother, Theo, came to see him.
Theo was an art dealer in Paris.
He was shocked to see how ill Vincent was.

The brothers were very close.
Theo had always understood Vincent
and supported him.

When Theo saw Vincent's drawings he said,
'You are an artist, Vincent!
You must paint.
I will give you money to live on.'
Vincent looked at Theo. He smiled.
Now he understood why he had failed
at his other jobs.
They were the wrong jobs.
He was going to be an artist.
He had found himself at last.

Vincent went back to Holland
to stay with his family.
He knew he needed proper art lessons.
He went to an artist's studio
and watched him work.

His family wanted Vincent to paint pictures
of rich people.
But Vincent didn't want to paint rich people.
He wanted to paint working people –
peasants who worked the land.

He showed his work to an art dealer.
But the art dealer didn't think much of it.
'This stuff will never sell,' he said.

But Vincent carried on painting.
He painted pictures of a prostitute, Christine.
He had met her in a cafe.
Vincent had never had much luck with women.
He always fell in love with women
who didn't love him.
He felt less lonely
when he was with Christine.
He asked her to marry him
and to his surprise she said yes.

But the marriage was a mistake.
They didn't really love each other.
Christine already had five children
by different men
and was expecting another by someone else.

She wasn't interested in Vincent's painting.
She thought he was wasting his time.
In the end, they split up.

Vincent threw himself into his painting.
He sent all his work to Theo in Paris.

Theo bought him oil paints and canvases.
Now Vincent could add colour to his figures.

'The Potato Eaters', painted in 1885

He painted the sun-bronzed faces
of the peasants in the fields.
He painted the dark golden yellow
of the cornfields.
He painted the dark deep blue
of the summer sky.

He made lots of sketches
of a family of peasants.
He sketched them working,
digging in the fields,
eating potatoes for their dinner.
Then he painted them in oil on canvas.
The painting was called 'The Potato Eaters'.
It showed the peasants in dark, dusty colours,
eating the supper they had dug
with their own hands.

And then Theo wrote from Paris,
asking Vincent to come and join him.
Vincent packed his bags and left for Paris.

6 Paris, 1886

At that time,
Paris was the centre of the art world.
Vincent got to know a group of artists there.
They were called the Impressionists
and used light colours in their work.
Many people laughed
at Impressionist painting.
They thought it looked half-finished.

But Vincent wanted to paint
like the Impressionists.
He made friends with them.
His close friend was another artist
called Paul Gauguin.

Vincent liked being with other artists
and talking about art.
And he loved being with Theo again.
But he found it hard to work in Paris.
He needed to be on his own again.
It was time to leave Paris.
He decided to go to the South of France.
He would have some peace and quiet there
and would be able to work.

'Terrace of the cafe in the evening', drawn in 1888

7 Sunflowers

As soon as Vincent got off the train
he could feel the heavy heat of the south.
The air was clear.
The golden yellow sun was bright
in the deep blue sky.
The river gleamed silver.
And there was a stillness.
The almond trees did not move.

It was as if the hot sun re-charged Vincent.
Now he had the energy to paint again.

The people in the town thought he was mad.
He would go out with no hat to protect him
from the sun.
He would work all day from sunset to sunrise.
He also worked at night.
He painted the bright cafes
and the clear midnight blue sky filled with stars.

Vincent could not stop painting.
He knew that Theo might not be able
to sell any of the paintings.
But he didn't care.
He painted because he loved it.
And it took his mind off his loneliness.

Then Vincent heard from Theo
that his friend Paul was ill.
He wrote to Paul and asked him
to come and stay.
Vincent thought they could work together.
They would send Theo a canvas
every month to sell in Paris.

Before Paul arrived,
Vincent painted pictures of sunflowers.
Lots and lots of pictures of bright yellow
sunflowers.
He put them all in Paul's room
to welcome him.

'What's all this?' said Paul when he arrived.
'Sunflowers,' said Vincent.
'Don't you like them?'
'Not much,' said Paul. 'Take them away.'

'Sunflowers', painted in 1889

8 The Razor

Vincent and Paul could not agree
about anything.
They had terrible rows all the time.
Paul said that Vincent
would never be a proper painter.

This made Vincent work even harder.
He painted in the fields
with the hot sun beating down on him.
It was as if the sun gave him extra energy.

Vincent and Paul would paint all day
and then have rows all night.
They didn't eat or sleep.
They spent all their money
on drink and smoking.

Paul had had enough of it.
He wanted to go back to Paris.

The night before he left, they went to a cafe.
Vincent did not have any money
to pay Rachel, a prostitute.
'It doesn't matter,' she laughed.
'Give me your ear.'

When Vincent got home he stood in front
of the sink.
He lifted his razor
and looked at his face in the mirror.

With one slash, he cut off his ear.
Blood poured into the sink.
He picked up his ear, washed it,
put it in some paper and took it to Rachel.

'Self-portrait with ear cut off', painted in 1889

9 Madness

Vincent went home and fell deeply asleep.
When he woke up, Paul had gone.

Vincent felt very ill.
It hurt where he had cut his ear off.
And he was suffering from sunstroke.
He heard voices in his head.
They spoke of madness and death.

Very soon, Vincent was known
throughout the whole town as a madman.
One day, he looked out of the window
and saw a gang of children shouting:
'Vincent! Vincent! Throw us your ear!'

Then Vincent went really mad.
He flung open the window and threw
everything he had at the children –
cups, plates, books, chairs,
even his beloved paintings.
The children ran away laughing.
But this was too much for the townspeople.
They were afraid of Vincent.

He was put into a mental hospital
where they told him
he was suffering from fits.
They said he needed rest.

What had his painting brought him?
Nothing.
He had never earned any money from it,
and now here he was in a mental hospital.

He was close to despair.
But then he got a letter from Theo.
Theo told him about Dr Gachet.
This doctor had seen Vincent's work
and understood his illness.
He thought he was a great artist.
He wanted to help Vincent.

So Vincent travelled to the north of France.
He stayed in a cafe near Dr Gachet's house.

Every day, he would go to the doctor's house
to paint.
But he didn't have the same energy
as before.
He felt burnt out.

He was afraid.
Theo wasn't well and could lose his job.
Also, Theo was married
and had his own family now.
Maybe he wouldn't be able
to send money to Vincent any more.
Vincent hated to be a burden to him.

What could Vincent do with his life?
Over the last year
he had kept himself alive
by painting.
But now he felt he couldn't go on.
And what if the terrible fits came back?

It was then, in July 1890,
that Vincent decided to shoot himself.

10 Theo and Vincent

'Vincent! Vincent!'

It was his brother's voice.
Vincent's eyes opened.
Here he was in his room.
The wound in his side was bandaged,
but the bandage was soaked with blood.
Theo was standing by the bed.

Theo's eyes filled with tears as he looked at
his brother.
Vincent knew he was close to death.

'You know, Vincent, one day your paintings
will be in galleries all over the world.
They will sell for millions.'

Vincent looked at his brother.
He smiled.
Theo had always believed in him.

It was one o'clock in the morning.
Vincent closed his eyes for the last time.

Key Dates

1853 Vincent van Gogh born in Holland

1874 Vincent goes to London to work
for an art dealer

1877 Vincent goes to work for the Church
in Belgium

1880 Vincent leaves the Church
and becomes a painter

1886 Vincent goes to Paris to paint.
He stays with Theo and meets the
Impressionists

1888 Vincent goes to the South of France
to paint

1889 Vincent becomes mentally ill
and is put in a mental hospital

1890 Vincent kills himself

1987 Vincent's painting 'Sunflowers' is sold
in London for £25 million